LEARY TALES

by

the Leary's

Copyright © 2022 the Leary's.
Cover Illustration: Jon Leary

All rights reserved. No part of this book may be reproduced, stored, or transmitted by any means—whether auditory, graphic, mechanical, or electronic—without written permission of both publisher and author, except in the case of brief excerpts used in critical articles and reviews. Unauthorized reproduction of any part of this work is illegal and is punishable by law.

ISBN: 979-8-88640-580-4 (sc)
ISBN: 979-8-88640-581-1 (hc)
ISBN: 979-8-88640-582-8 (e)

Because of the dynamic nature of the Internet, any web addresses or links contained in this book may have changed since publication and may no longer be valid. The views expressed in this work are solely those of the author and do not necessarily reflect the views of the publisher, and the publisher hereby disclaims any responsibility for them.

One Galleria Blvd., Suite 1900, Metairie, LA 70001
1-888-421-2397

A Man Named Bob

My favorite artist was a man named Bob
Whenever he painted, he attracted a mob
His favorite dish....corn on the cob
Not a kernel left, he wasn't a slob!

I'd go down to the village and watch him paint
I learned later he was also a saint
He gave me free lessons, as I watched and stared
Others were in awe of how much he cared.

Now when I paint I try to do a good job
I remember my favorite artist named Bob
How he took his time and would never rush
Mixing colors with his magical brush!

                                                        Artist Ben Poet Jan

Fussy Old Goat

I had some sauce, I gave it a toss
It went down the throat, of a fussy old goat
He started to spit, but the sauce wouldn't quit
Shaking his head with a crazy kick
It was on his beard, and he gave a lick

It wasn't a joke, when he started to choke
I hit him on the back, and he started to hack
It wasn't a hassle, when he went to the castle
He swam across the moat, he could have taken a boat!

When he got on the ground, he was chased by a hound
He went back to his hut, with a very sore butt
When he went to his house, he saw his goat spouse
"Where were you she said"?
He didn't say, he just went to bed!

Artist Jon Poet Bob

Autumn Tree

The leaves on the trees are falling
Looks to me winter is calling
Red, orange, yellow and brown
Don't be upset or make a frown!

But winter is long and sometimes boring
The trees need to rest, so they are snoring
But it's cold and bleak and not so much fun
Well don't complain, you can still see the sun.

You can ski, and sled or go for a walk
Build an igloo, laugh, sing and talk
Old Jack Frost is nothing to fear
Before you know it; spring will be here!

Artist Ben Poet Jan

Catching Air

I can do ollies and catch a lot of air
I do it with style, grace and flair
I have no problem spinning and flipping
My suction cup feet are great for gripping

If you need a good teacher, I know that I'm good
At least this is what I have understood
I practice every day to become the best
So far my skills have past every test

So if you don't have a clue of what you are doing
And skateboarding is something you are pursuing
Look me up any time you've got a moment to spare
I'll be out and about catching some air!

Artist Jon Poet Jan

My Dad Loves Coffee

My dad drinks coffee sip, gulp, slurp
He laughs a little and lets out a burp
On the phone, in the car, and at the supper table
He drinks any coffee, no matter the label

Smoke signals are in the air when its burning hot
Or a whip cream tower when he lays on his cot
When he's nervous and scratching his head in concern
Sometimes in the micro his coffee will burn

Outside playing baseball he places it on the side
I can smell it at home plate when I slide
He drinks a lot, and I have to laugh
He always says regular and not decaf!

Artist Ben Poet Jan

Little Robot

I had a little robot
Th at was as colorful as candy
With all that he could do
Th is guy was really handy!

He could call my sister
Play a CD or wash the dishes
I could just relax
While he accomplished all my wishes!

Artist Ben Poet Jan

Quarter Pipe

A quarter pipe is really where it's at you know
Your way up high, then down you go
It's like riding a wave that doesn't move
But somehow you know you're in the groove

You can start at the bottom with an itty bitty slide
Then take it to the top where I'm sure you'll glide
Your elbow and knee pads hug your limbs so tight
A helmet for your head and there's no more fright!

So take it from the top and take a deep breath in
Let your skateboard move off the rim
As your flying down lean forward not back
Enjoy your adventure, you're on the right track!

Artist Ben Poet Jan

Hank the Crank!

There was a fellow named "Hank the Crank"
He talked to himself and had money in the bank
Checking his account there was a very big gain
"Not enough" he said, and began to complain.

He got in his car all shiny and bright
Then he noticed a scratch near the headlight
Driving out to a farm in the countryside
Hank just needed a place to hide!

Entering a barn he saw a horse and a cow
"I want to be happy, please tell me how?"
Mr. Cow told him to go feed the chickens and hens
"Then you'll be happy, you'll have new friends"!

Artist Jon Poet Bob

Crocky

I thought Crocky
Was off his rocky
He had a red and white hat
And he was sort of fat

He was wide eyed and kooky
Even a bit spooky
He laughed so loud
He was drawing a crowd

But what I found amazing
As his blue skateboard was blazing
Was his never ending bag of tricks
Crocky sure knew how to get his kicks!

                                                    Artist Ben Poet Jan

Jazz Musician

I knew a jazz musician
Th at played very good
He was the best around,
Now that was understood!

He would be bop and boo beep
And tap his feet up and down
He was always happy playing with a smile,
Not a frown!

Two tennis balls seemed to be stuck in his cheeks
And out of the horn were grunts, groans and squeaks
With his cool little hat and his round little glasses
He had a sound that was sweet as molasses!

Artist Ben Poet Bob

Little Lamb

Little lamb standing in a field
Cute and cuddly, with great appeal
Maybe I'll ask him to go for a walk
Then I remembered he can't talk

I saw a bees nest and had to scram
No time to be calm like little lamb
One whose fleece is very white
As for me I'll go fly a kite

It's fun to do things you like
Like jumping rope and riding a bike
Tonight when it's time to go to sleep
I'll rest on my pillow and count some sheep!

Artist Jon Poet Bob

Basketball

I like to dribble a basketball
I only wish that I was tall
It's fun to play on any court
Basketball is my favorite sport!

I like to pass but I'd rather shoot
But anyway the point is moot
My friend and I play one on one
We run and jump and have some fun.

Pretending we're either Lakers or Knicks
We even practice setting picks
What would make my life complete
Is if I were only seven feet!

Artist Ben Poet Bob

Blue City

I dreamt that everything I saw was blue
So many stairs that I didn't know what to do
Boxes, windows and funny circles to boot
So many places it was quite the hoot!

I thought I saw a turtle wearing a top hat
And then I thought I saw a little rat!
Fish tails, monograms, E's and T's
So much excitement I had to sneeze!

I woke up and left my strange blue city
I left it behind, it was quite a pity
No more boxes, doors, or funny funnels
No more getting lost in the deep blue tunnels!

Artist Ben Poet Jan

Pteranodon

I thought I saw
A large dinosaur
It flew in the air
And gave me a scare

Bigger than a swan
It was a pteranodon
With wings large and wide
I needed a place to hide

Landing on the rocky ground
The huge bird looked around
Then strutting and looking very proud
Pteranodon disappeared into a cloud!

Artist Jon PoetBob

Fred the Egg

Edgar the Egg had a brother named Fred
Who didn't roll, but bounced instead
Up and down he would go
Fred was very hard boiled you know

At the family reunion it was quite a sight
With eggs cracking jokes into the night
Fred laughed loud and started to ramble
He had to make sure he didn't scramble

The brothers sometimes liked to boast
Usually at breakfast eating burnt toast
All the eggs were leaving, it was getting late
They had to be sure not to end up on a plate!

Artist Ben Poet Bob

What's Up?

I heard a ssss when I turned around
I didn't want to make one little sound
Is it a cat? Is it a pup?
No it's a snake and he said, "What's Up"?

Black sunglasses covered his eyes
I thought to myself, "What a disguise"!
A tiny red tongue that slipped in and out
"What's Up"? He said in a boisterous shout!

I laughed and stared in unbelief
"What's Up"? he yelled, this time with grief
"I don't know, I'm in shock, I was a little abrupt
"I guess I never heard a snake say, "What's Up"?!

Artist Jon Poet Jan

What Is This Bird?

Have you heard
About the bird
Was it a raven
Looking for a haven

Or a large osprey
Th at lost his way
A red tailed hawk
Who began to squawk

A blue tailed swallow
Needing someone to follow
It was an eagle going home
Th at's the way to end this poem!

                                                Artist Jon Poet Bob

Golf

In golf you hope to always make par
First you need to hit it far
Whether with a wood or an iron
You smack the ball and send it flying

Hope the ball goes long and straight
Or landing in a hazard will be your fate
It could be water or a deep sand trap
Pay attention listen to this rap

Then take aim and shoot for the flag
If you land close no need to brag
Now a nice easy stroke right at the hole
When it lands in the cup you've reached your goal!

Artist Ben Poet Bob

Is It an Izzy?

Is it an Izzy or is it a Lizzy?
It sailed on by like it was busy
"Are you from Jupiter or are you from Mars"?
He rode on by as fast as the cars.

"I'm not from neither", I heard him yell
Making a sharp turn he almost fell
"Well where are you from"? I yelled back in haste.
But he seemed like he didn't have a minute to waste!

"Are you from Saturn or maybe the moon"?
Are you from Venus or perhaps Neptune"?
"I'm not from neither he said with a sigh
"Pluto's my home and I'm just passing by"!

Artist Jon Poet Jan

Manny the Moose

Manny the moose
Was on the loose
He took a caboose
But that's no excuse

On a trip downtown
He looked all around
The city lights were pretty
Manny loved the city!

With all the noise, it was a riot
Manny longed for peace and quiet
But it wasn't in vain
He returned home to Maine!

                                                Artist Jon Poet Bob

Sledding

The golf course is a great place to sled
It sure beats staying home in bed
Sliding down a mountain of snow
It's fun to see how fast I'll go.

My dog always barks when I go by
Maybe he wants to give it a try
I huff and I puff going up the hill
But when I slide down it's quite the thrill!

It's fun outside with all my friends
Taking curves around the bends
Winter is no time to stay inside
When you can enjoy this roller coaster ride!

Artist Jon Poet Jan

Soccer

Sign up for soccer if you like to run
By the end of the game your physically done
If both teams are matched perfectly the same
Then you are in for an exciting game!

It will be up the field; down the field with this black and white ball,
Occasionally the players tumble and fall,
In the bleachers heads are turning left and right
Both teams are putting up a good fight.

A strategic kick will place the ball in the net
A head butt does the same, so don't you fret
At bed time you'll have no problem snoozing
Unless you were the team that wound up losing!

Artist Jon Poet Jan

My Calico Cat

I had a calico cat with eyes of green
She was the slyest hunter I have ever seen
She would sneak and pounce on all her prey
Though they wiggled and squiggled they could not get away!

She loved to eat bugs and you could hear them crunch
Every day it seemed she would have them for lunch
Beatles, grass hoppers and little flies she would eat
She thought all these insects were delicious treats!

Artist Ben Poet Jan

The Jester

I saw a jester at a fair
His funny hat covered his hair
A quirky shuffle; a funny dance
His silly hops so happenstance

He had little bells on his hat, legs and pants
Everyone enjoyed his yakkety yakkety rants
His little wand moved up and down
While the balls circled without a sound

The Jester announced "King Richard was coming"!
He did another dance with a little humming
He gave me a wink from the corner of his eye
This strange looking man was anything but shy!

Artist Jon Poet Jan

The Ring

I was walking down the street
Playing with my ring,
All of a sudden it dropped
And I head a "Ping"!

It rolled down the street
So I started to run
It rolled faster and faster
I thought "This isn't fun"!

It rolled over ant hills
It rolled over a car
It rolled over tin cans
It rolled really far!

It finally hit a tree in a nearby park,
I reached and grabbed it; and I was home before dark!

Artist Jon Poet Jan

Winter

Summer is over, Autumn leaves are gold
Next comes Winter when it gets cold
Snow and sleet make it hard to play
Why even the birds have to fly away!

I'll just have to do the best I can
"Lets' have some fun", said a tall snowman
He went to the pond and began to skate
Turning and gliding he made a fi gure eight.

He was having a ball skating on the ice
I started to smile and said, "Th is is nice"!
"Now", said the snowman, "Do you understand"?
"That this season can be a winter wonderland"!

Artist Jon Poet Bob

The Mood for Food

I was sitting and watching the tele
I got up to feed my belly
A nice sandwich peanut butter and jelly
It tasted good, it wasn't smelly!

What I needed was something to drink
Juice or soda, what do you think?
A nice big glass of cold lemonade
Th is will make my thirst start to fade

Time for dessert lets' not forget
Pie or cake I won't regret
Now I'm full until much later
Thank you Mom for the "Refrigerator"!

Artist Ben Poet Bob

Willie the Whale

One bright sunny day it occurred to me
I'd take my boat and go out to sea
I started to fi sh when I noticed a tail
It belonged to a creature named Willie the Whale

Willie said, "Hi what brings you here"?
"Why not", I said, "on a day so clear"
He jumped, dived, and put on a show
Diving in the water, made the wind blow

Waving goodbye, I headed to shore
Time for a visit to the candy store
It might sound strange or even silly
Sometimes I sure miss my friend named Willie!

Artist Jon Poet Bob

The Butterfly

A butterfly is an awesome bug
When it's very young it crawls like a slug
A Monarch is my favorite it's orange and black
Sometimes when it flutters; it lands on my back

I chase after it with a very fi ne net
I'm gonna get it so I won't fret
I catch him by his wings and stare into his eyes
He looks like he says, "Hey pick on someone your own size"!

Artist Ben Poet Jan

Firefighter

Woooooooooooooooo this horn was loud and clear
Everyone knew the fi re engine was really near
Swoooooooooooooooooosh as the water left the hose
Oh my! Th is building looked like a fi ery rose!

After many hours went by
Finally we could see the sky
Everything looked very wet
I just loved their dalmation pet!

Artist Ben Poet Jan

Edgar the Egg

Edgar the Egg
Never had to beg
He couldn't leap, he didn't walk
Or sing, or dance or even talk

But he would roll around like a ball
With a great big smile for one and all
Across the meadows, past the cows
There were no moos, only wows!

Lions can roar, hippos can swim
Edgar was different there was no one like him
He could roll on grass and the street
With his own style that was hard to beat

Edgars' shell didn't crack, break or dent
Because Edgar the egg was egg-cellent!

Artist Ben Poet Bob

Pirate Ship

In the middle of the night I let out a scream
I saw a pirate ship in my dream
The skeleton head looked a little undaunted
I didn't see pirates but perhaps it was haunted!

"Calm down little man, what you saw wasn't real",
Said my father with a smile as he began to kneel
"We'll fix this bad dream once and for all
God takes care of the big and even the small"!

So with one little prayer I began to snooze
A new adventure; a different cruise
But I never will forget that deep blue ocean
And the scary ship that had no motion!

Artist Jon Poet Jan

Spenderella

There was a very happy fella
Who had a wife named Spenderella
Every day it happened without fail
She'd go to the mall in search of a sale

It didn't matter what kind of store
She only knew she wanted more
Some prices are low, and some are high
No matter the cost she was sure to buy

At Christmas time when bells would ring
She could make those cash registers sing
Late at night when shops would close
You could hear her say, "I'll take one of those"!

Artist Ben Poet Bob

Funny Penguins

Funny penguins do a flip
Standing on ice they start to slip
Turning around they make a wish
Then reach right down to catch a fish

Even though the water is so cold
They jump right in because they're bold
The sun is rising a new day has begun
Penguins love to laugh, talk and have fun

How sharp they are in a shiny black coat
Swimming along, diving, and then a back float
Yes the penguins are cute and oh so nice
Happy as clams in their world of ice!

Artist Ben Poet Bob

A Bright Sunny Day

A sunny day and the wind is right
I think I'll go and fly a kite
First I need to fi nd some string
Then I'll be able to do my thing

I brought my kite down to the beach
Very soon it was out of reach
Soaring above in the great blue sky
Amazing that this kite can fly

The sun was shining oh so bright
The kite disappeared out of sight
I couldn't even say a word
Perhaps my kite became a bird!

Artist Ben Poet Bob

Baseball

I love to catch, hit and run
Baseball is a game that's really fun
I have to be sure to tie my laces
Or I'll be tripping around the bases

swing my bat when the pitcher throws
Is it a curve or a slider; only he knows
When the umpire yells "strike three you're out"!
If it's the other team the fans really shout!

Sometimes I go see the games with my Dad
If my team loses I won't be sad
Not winning a game is no good reason
Because they'll always be another season!

Artist Ben Poet Bob

Circular Paths

I like to doodle when I'm on the phone
I do it a lot when I'm at home
Circles and curves that go round and round
Squiggly lines that look like mounds

I picture myself walking in the tunnels
Many of these look like funnels
Running and racing in a circular path
Falling in holes, then I'm home at last!

Artist Ben Poet Jan

Danny the Dolphin

Danny Dolphin loved to swim
Even more than his friend Jim
Out of the water he would leap
Then down again into the deep

Using flippers he'd surf a wave
He was fast and very brave
Moving around always in motion
Danny ruled the bright blue ocean

Either the Atlantic or Pacific
He really wasn't that specific
His body was long and sleek
If you got up close he'd kiss your cheek!

Artist Ben Poet Bob

Now I Lay Me Down to Sleep

Now I lay me down to sleep
Lord, if your there please make a peep!
My bear and I want to say goodnight
In fact we'd like to hold you tight!

We're grateful and thankful for all we own
If we could say it to you quicker we'd use the phone
Please take care of my Mom and Dad
And help me to never be really bad.

Tomorrow, please make the sun shine brighter
Help Mommy to lose weight, she wants to be lighter
Help Daddy not to lose any more of his hair
I only have one baseball cap he could wear.

Artist Ben Poet Jan

Hot Air Balloon

One day about noon
I went up in a hot air balloon
It was so much fun
In the sky with the sun.

We saw some birds just flying by
They also seemed to love the sky
It was amazing having a birds' eye view
I never did this, it was totally new

So now when I think of that special day
I think of my Dad and how much he had to pay
But for once in a lifetime, it didn't seem that bad
But we emptied my piggy bank of everything I had!

Artist Ben Poet Jan

Ducks Life

Sometimes when I'm out of luck
I wish I could be a duck
Warm and happy as a lark
Swimming in a pond till after dark

Winter or summer I don't care
Ducks don't worry what to wear
My clothes might get all scruffy
But ducks are always soft and fluffy

It's fun to watch them fly around
Then flap their wings and hit the ground
Time to go home now but I'll be back
To visit my friends who "Quack, Quack, Quack"!

Artist Ben Poet Bob

Freddy the Fox

A cute little fox sly and ready
I guess I'll have to call him Freddy
What's that red flower near his nose?
Now I see it must be a rose!

"Excuse me", I said, "I beg your pardon!
What are you doing walking in my garden?
Shouldn't you be in the woods at play,
Running, jumping and dancing in the hay"?

"He said, "I like to venture out now and then,
Go on a hike and perhaps meet a friend.
In fact I thought it would be exquisite,
To come right over and pay you a visit"!

Artist Ben Poet Bob

Gadgets and Wadgets

I'm a technology buff I collect all sorts of gadgets
I pods, t.v.'s, speakers, computers and wadgets
Coffee makers, screens, c.d's galore
And still for some reason, I always want more!

Monitors, keyboards, radio's and clickers
To find and label them, I think I need stickers
In a great big ball they all seem to be
I sometimes get lost; but at least I find me!

Artist Ben Poet Jan

Night Owls

It was late at night and very dark
I looked out my window just for a lark
Up in a tree to my surprise
Looking back at me were four yellow eyes

One seemed to frown or maybe scowl
Of course this had to be an owl
"Why are you sitting in that tree"?
"We're looking for food, and it's easier to see!"

When all of us are safe in bed
Th at's the time owls need to be fed
They are so alert and extremely wise
I yawned again and closed my eyes

Artist Ben Poet Bob

One Day in Court

What a thrill, what a sport
One day we all appeared in court
In fact we were grounded
The charges against us, were totally unfounded

Into the chamber came the judge
He gave us a wink, and then a nudge
What would happen next remained to be seen
All the lawyers had visions of green

Reporters swarmed around in a fury
Everyone wanted to talk to the jury
"Innocent" they said, "You know it's no crime
To exchange 2 nickels for 1 dime"!

Artist Ben Poet Bob

Little Shawn

I saw a dog once on the lawn
It was said his name was little Shawn
He romped and ran, jumped and played
He'd jump and hop, pounce and dance
He just loved to play, and bite the plants.

But then one day he fell in the sewer
Now the neighbors have one dog fewer
He struggled and swam but he floated away
He paddled and struggled ending up there in the bay.

A policeman spotted the little mutt
Reached in and grabbed him by the butt
Pulled him free and sent him home
Now that dog will no more roam!

Artist Jon Poet (Grandfather) Paul Winslow

Sailing Down the Nile

While sailing down the river Nile
I met a large floating crocodile
I didn't know if he was mean
Taking no chances I split the scene

Steering the boat over to land
I stepped out on blazing sand
The crocodile was behind me, trying to follow
Taking a deep breath, I tried to swallow

In the distance was a great pyramid
What a place to hide for a little kid
Old crocky had stopped the chase
Lying in an oasis splashing his face!

Artist Ben Poet Bob

Snakes!

I saw something move on the ground
Coming closer then I looked down
One was green another one brown
I couldn't believe what I had found!

They saw me too and tried to hide
Moving so fast they seemed to glide
A slip and slide and then a squiggle
I began to laugh and let out a giggle

They headed towards a tiny hole
Around a corner and over a knoll
"Stop"! I said, "for heavens' sakes"!
It's never easy to catch little snakes!

Artist Ben Poet Bob

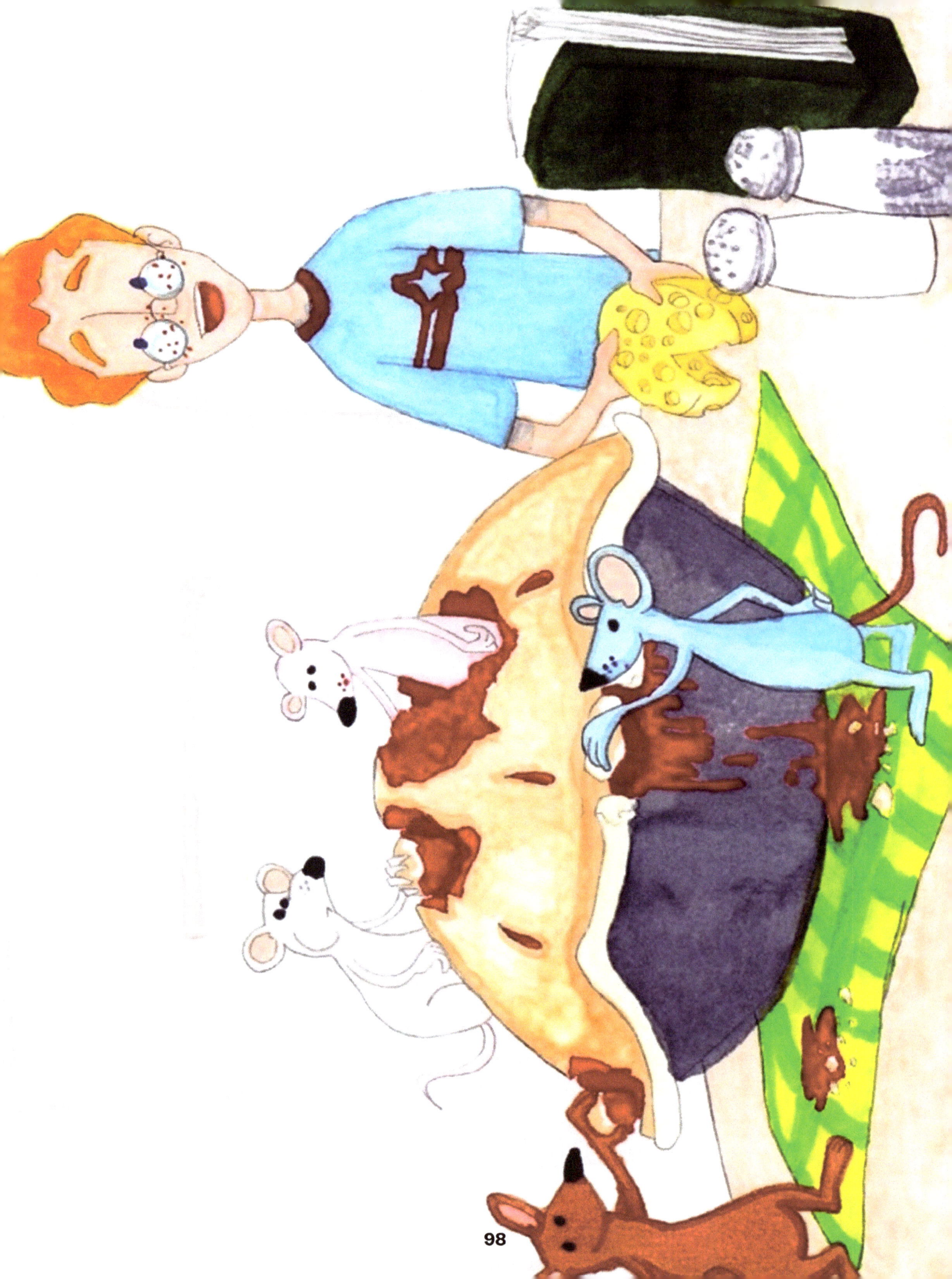

What a Riot!

Another day and every things quiet
How did I know there would be a riot
Looking around in every room
I heard a crash and then a boom

In the kitchen much to my surprise
I saw four mice eating apple pies
They were brown, blue, pink and grey
I didn't know what to think or say

Then one spoke and said, "If you please,
Could you get us some more cheese"?
When this mess is clean I'll feel better
Opening the fridge, I got them some cheddar!

Artist Ben Poet Bob

Circus

I sat at my desk in search of a new job
"I'm great with people, I'm not a snob!
I lift up their spirits and make them smile,
To forget about life and relax for a while.

I've looked here and there, no matter where I went
But my true calling is under the big tent!
I'll soon be happy, I don't mean to frown,
Have you heard the news... the Circus is in town!

Artist Ben Poet Bob

Take a Hike

I love to walk and go for a Hike!
It's even better than riding a bike!
The Peace and beauty is hard to beat
When you're strolling in silence on your feet

In the woods or on the beach
The beauty of nature is within your reach
No matter the place, time or season,
To explore God's creation, you don't need a reason!

                                                          Artist Ben Poet Jan

www.ingramcontent.com/pod-product-compliance
Lightning Source LLC
LaVergne TN
LVHW072126060526
838201LV00071B/4985